PREHISTORIC PEOPLE OF NORTH AMERICA

THE JUNIOR LIBRARY OF
AMERICAN INDIANS

PREHISTORIC PEOPLE OF NORTH AMERICA

Diana Childress

CHELSEA JUNIORS ❦

a division of CHELSEA HOUSE PUBLISHERS

ON THE COVER: A model of a Mississippian village showing two temple mounds and several houses. A new temple is being built.

FRONTISPIECE: Scientists excavate an 11,000 year old mammoth skeleton in southern Arizona.

CHAPTER TITLE ORNAMENT: A drawing of an eagle-shaped copper ornament, which was found in a Hopewell burial mound in Mound City, Ohio.

English-language words that are italicized in the text can be found in the glossary at the back of the book.

Chelsea House Publishers
EDITORIAL DIRECTOR Richard Rennert
EXECUTIVE MANAGING EDITOR Karyn Gullen Browne
COPY CHIEF Robin James
PICTURE EDITOR Adrian G. Allen
CREATIVE DIRECTOR Robert Mitchell
ART DIRECTOR Joan Ferrigno
PRODUCTON MANAGER Sallye Scott

The Junior Library of American Indians
SENIOR EDITOR Martin Schwabacher

Staff for PREHISTORIC PEOPLE OF NORTH AMERICA
EDITORIAL ASSISTANT Erin McKenna
ASSISTANT DESIGNER Stephen Schildbach
PICTURE RESEARCHER Sandy Jones

3 5 7 9 8 6 4 2

Library of Congress Cataloging-in-Publication Data

Childress, Diana.
Prehistoric People of North America / Diana Childress.
  p. cm. — (The Junior Library of American Indians)
Includes index.
        0-7910-2481-4
        0-7910-2482-2 (pbk.)
1. Paleo-Indians—North America—Juvenile literature. 2. Indians of North America—Origin—Juvenile literature. 3. Indians of North America—Antiquities—Juvenile literature. 4. North America—Antiquities—Juvenile literature. [1. Indians of North America—Antiquities. 2. Man, Prehistoric. 3. North America—Antiquities. 4. Archaeology.] I. Title. II. Series.
E77.92.048 1996   95-31636
970.01—dc20   CIP
                                                      AC

CONTENTS

An 1850 painting of the inside
of a mound being excavated by
Dr. Montroville Dickeson. In the
19th century, Dickeson dug up
about 1,000 mounds and
carried off 40,000 artifacts..

CHAPTER 1

Discovering the Past

In 1780, Thomas Jefferson, the governor of Virginia and future president of the United States, set out to unravel a mystery. Virginia's landscape was dotted with large man-made hills. The mounds of earth were known to contain human bones, but no one knew who had built the mounds or for what reason.

Jefferson looked for answers by investigating a 12-foot mound near his home. In his book *Notes on the State of Virginia,* Jefferson described his *excavation:* "I first dug superficially in several parts of it, and came to collections of human bones, at different depths, from six inches to three feet below the surface." The bones, some of adults, some of children, were jumbled together as if they had been carried there and emptied from a basket.

Jefferson then cut a path through the mound "wide enough for a man to walk through and examine its sides." He discovered four distinct layers of bones, separated by soil and stones from a nearby river. He estimated that about 1,000 skeletons lay in the mound, and that the bones had been collected and placed there at four different times. The information he gathered led Jefferson to conclude that prehistoric Indians had built the mounds as burial sites for their dead.

With his careful excavation and detailed report, Thomas Jefferson became one of the first people to take a scientific approach to the study of the prehistory of Native Americans.

Prehistory is the history of people who did not leave written records. Native Americans who lived north of Mexico did not have a system of writing, so events that occurred in this area before the arrival of European explorers in the 16th century are considered prehistoric. Scientists must use a variety of methods to learn about the past and to assemble a picture of prehistoric American life.

Much of this picture has been provided by early explorers and missionaries who wrote descriptions of the people they encountered. Their reports contain valuable information about the ways in which Native Americans lived before their *cultures* were altered by contact with Europeans. Native Americans have also supplied information about their history through the stories that have been passed down through the generations. These traditions do not, however, reach back far enough to explain how the Indians first came to America.

Even in Thomas Jefferson's day, the origins of the Native Americans were a subject of debate. Some people looked for answers in the Old Testament of the Bible or in the writings of the ancient Greeks and Romans. But Jefferson thought that the physical similarities between American Indians and eastern Asians were an important clue. Today physical anthropologists study these racial relationships by looking at bones, teeth, and blood types of early people.

Jefferson also believed that languages give valuable evidence about the past. When groups of people split up and move apart, each group develops its own way of speaking. Centuries later, these groups will speak different languages. By comparing

Archaeologists excavate Wilson Butte Cave in Idaho. For thousands of years, the cave provided shelter for prehistoric Indians. Some of the oldest human remains in America have been found here.

the words and grammar of these languages, linguists can discover similarities that reveal their shared history.

The richest information about the first Americans comes from the objects that they left behind. Such objects include the timbers, hearths, and post holes that remain from ancient dwellings; tools; baskets; pots; scraps of clothing; and human and animal bones. Scientists who examine these objects in order to understand the lives of the people who once used them are called *archaeologists.*

Archaeologists have many ways of figuring out the age of ancient objects. One method is based on the simple idea that the upper layers of the earth's surface were laid on top of the lower layers and therefore must be more recent. If an area has not been disturbed, the deeper archaeologists dig, the older any items they find will be. They must keep track of the layers of a dig in order to know which items belong to the same period of time. For this reason they dig carefully with hand tools such as shovels, trowels, and even brushes. Digging systematically and labeling each layer is called stratigraphy.

To determine the approximate age of each layer and of the artifacts found in it, archaeologists must know something about the *geology* of the site being excavated. Often, however, sites cannot be dated solely by geological information. Sometimes people, animals, or nature have already disturbed the site, removing important evidence that reveals its age. For example, along the Porcupine River in Canada's Yukon Territory, floods and erosion have so churned up the soil that 1,400-year-old bone tools were found buried in layers of earth that are 350,000 years old.

When archaeologists come across the remains of plants and animals, they have a special means of finding out their age. All living things contain carbon atoms, and a small fraction of this carbon is radioactive carbon, or carbon 14. When a plant or animal dies, the carbon 14 begins to decay at a steady rate, called a half-life.

The half-life of carbon 14 is about 5,730 years. That means that in 5,730 years, the amount of carbon 14 in a sample will be reduced by one half. In twice that time—11,460 years—the carbon 14 will be halved again, so only one quarter of the original amount will remain. By comparing the amount of carbon 14 in the air today with the amount in objects found in an archaeological dig, scientists can date materials that come from living things, such as wood, charcoal, bones, wool, linen, cotton, silk, leather, fur, seeds, and pollen. This method, known as radiocarbon dating, is very reliable for determining dates within the last 50,000 years.

Trees offer another calendar by keeping a diary of the weather. When a tree is cut, its trunk reveals a pattern of rings. Each of these rings represents one year of growth in the life of the tree. Because the amount of growth each year is determined by weather

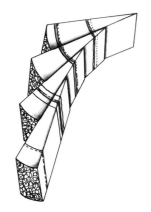

Using dendrochronology, archaeologists can date ancient wood by comparing its tree-ring patterns with the patterns of other pieces of wood.

conditions, trees produce wide rings in rainy years and narrow rings in dry years. All trees living in the same region have a similar pattern of thick and thin rings because they have lived through the same periods of rain and drought.

By comparing the rings of a newly cut tree with the rings in older pieces of wood, scientists can find out the age of the older wood. For example, if a 200-year-old tree is cut down, years can be applied to each ring by counting backward in time from the outermost ring, which was created in the last year of the tree's life. If the rings of this tree are compared with those of a timber used in a 150-year-old house, the ring patterns of the two pieces of wood will overlap. Scientists can determine when the older tree was cut down and extend the calendar of rings further back in time. If the pattern of that timber is compared with an even older piece of wood that has an overlapping pattern, the time line is extended further. For the American Southwest and other areas where periodic droughts leave dramatic ring patterns, scientists have made charts of patterns reaching back more than 8,000 years. Tree dating, or dendrochronology, can pinpoint the exact year a tree was cut down to build a prehistoric home.

When archaeologists discover the remnants of ancient hearths, they can figure out the age of the site through their understanding of the earth's *magnetic field.* When a compass needle points north, it is not pointing directly to the earth's north pole, but rather to the north pole of the earth's magnetic field. Similarly, when iron particles in clay are heated by a fire, they point toward the magnetic north pole. When the clay cools, the iron particles are frozen in that position, even though the magnetic north pole continually changes its position. If an ancient hearth was built on soil that contained clay, the iron particles in the clay point toward the magnetic north pole of the era when people built fires there. Experts who know the history of the pole's movement can determine when the hearths were made. This method of dating is called archaeomagnetism.

Since dating methods usually give approximate rather than exact dates, archaeologists use as many techniques as possible before assigning an age to a site. That age may change as scientists devise new and improved ways of dating ancient materials.

Dating a site and its artifacts is only the beginning. Archaeologists also "read" the material evidence to learn about the people who created it. They examine ancient tools to determine whether they were weapons for hunting, stones for grinding grain into flour, knives for butchering animals, or some other device. Human bones reveal how long people lived and some of the diseases that afflicted them. Similar shapes of knives or pots found in different sites might indicate that people moved from one site to the other or that the people who lived in those areas traded goods or shared knowledge.

Prehistory resembles a jigsaw puzzle with many missing pieces. Much of the past remains to be uncovered, and scientists often disagree about the age and the significance of objects brought to light after centuries underground. Fortunately the incompleteness of the picture does not discourage students of prehistory. As one archaeologist has commented, "Archaeologists particularly love uncertainty, for every discovery is a challenging mix of ancient data and new interpretation at the same time."

Even though the puzzle remains unfinished, archaeologists have revealed the broad outlines of how the first humans arrived in the Americas and populated the "New World." ▲

The Ice Age hunters who crossed from Siberia to Alaska survived the harsh environment through their ingenuity in using what resources they could find. Pictured here is a reconstruction of a Siberian Ice Age house made of mammoth bones.

CHAPTER 2

The Ice Age Hunters

Twenty-five thousand years ago, the Pleistocene Epoch, or Ice Age, was nearly over. For more than 1.5 million years, several periods of extreme cold had enveloped the earth. One last freeze, called the late Wisconsin, was beginning to take place.

During the Ice Age vast sheets of ice, called *glaciers*, covered about one-third of the earth's surface. Because much of the world's water was frozen in these ice sheets, the level of the oceans dropped dramatically. Shelves of land that today lie far underwater were exposed. Between

Alaska and Siberia, a broad expanse of land emerged, connecting North America and Asia.

This territory, today called Beringia, became a grassy plain. In spite of bitter winters, sweltering summers, and little rainfall, this flat, treeless land provided rich grazing pastures for a variety of animals. Woolly mammoths and mastodons, three-ton ground sloths, horses, camels, tapirs, long-horned bison, and other plant-eating giants roamed the landscape. Their presence attracted predators such as panthers, lions, saber-toothed tigers, dire wolves, and short-nosed bears.

Bands of hunters who had learned to survive the rigors of the Siberian climate most likely discovered Beringia as they expanded their hunting ranges eastward. This wide plain full of animals must have seemed an earthly paradise. Skilled at hunting and Arctic living, bands spread across Beringia, eventually reaching what is now Alaska. These early Americans are known as Paleo-Indians.

No one knows exactly when these Ice Age hunters set foot in America. Some archaeologists believe they have found evidence that humans lived in the Americas as far back as 20,000 or 30,000 years ago. But not all scientists accept the accuracy of these very early dates. The oldest human-made stone tools that can be reliably dated were found at Bluefish Cave in the Canadian Yukon. These tools are thought to be between 12,000 and 15,000 years old.

During the time that Beringia remained above sea level, two thick sheets of ice covered most of Canada. Paleo-Indians were unable to migrate southward from Alaska and northwestern Canada until the world's climate began to grow warmer around 14,000 years ago. As the Ice Age drew to an end, the glaciers began to melt and the sea level rose. Little by little, over a period of 3,000 to 4,000 years, most of Beringia disappeared underwater. The land bridge between Asia and America ceased to exist.

At some time during this long warming, a passageway opened between the two major North American glaciers. Bold pioneers discovered this open corridor along the Mackenzie River valley. Past "frigid glacial lakes and tumultous rivers," through "bogs, deltas, spurs of ice, and barren landscapes" (as one archaeologist imagines it), they hiked southward into the Great Plains of Canada and the United States.

After enduring the extreme conditions of Beringia and the treacherous journey bet-

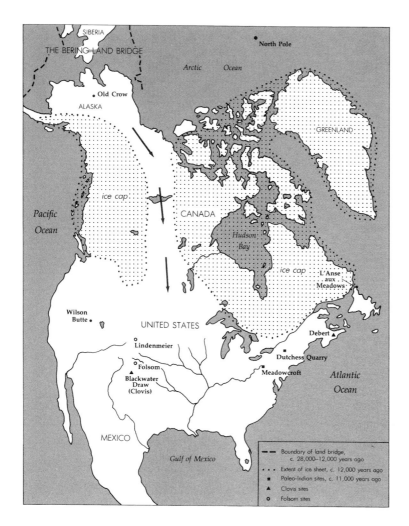

This map of North America shows the possible route of the Paleo-Indians as they crossed into Alaska and gradually spread across the continent and into South America.

ween melting glaciers, the Paleo-Indians must have welcomed the warm, wet climate of late Ice Age America. Large numbers of animals unused to human predators supplied them with ample meat, skins for clothing and tents, and bones for tools. With plentiful food and wide spaces to roam, these early Americans prospered, rapidly growing in number and spreading across the land.

One archaeologist points out that even if a single hunting band of only 25 people had passed through the Mackenzie corridor, they could have been the ancestors of all Native Americans. For if the population of this band had doubled every generation (that is, every 30 years or so), in 500 years the population would have swelled to more than 10 million people. In those 500 years, these far-ranging *nomads* would only have to move about 16 miles a year to expand from southern Canada to the southernmost tip of South America.

The first evidence that humans lived in America during the Ice Age was discovered in 1926. Several years earlier, a cowboy in New Mexico had noticed some bones sticking out of the ground. These bones were much larger than those of cows or any other animals living in the area. Paleontologists (people who study fossils) identified the bones as belonging to a type of bison that lived in North America during the Ice Age. When a team of scientists began digging up the bones, they found spearheads among them and realized that the bison had been killed by Ice Age hunters. Since this discovery archaeologists have found many sites with similar tools dating from 10,000 to 11,500 years ago. Together these sites show that a hunting culture spread rapidly across North America and into South America.

Paleo-Indian tools include knives, scrapers to clean hides, spokeshaves to shape wooden shafts for spears and lances, and gravers to pierce hides and cut slots in bone or antler. Spear-throwers, or atlatls, are special sticks about 20 inches long with a hooked end. They enabled hunters to throw their spears with greater force.

Many of these tools resemble artifacts found in Siberia. Only in America, however, have archaeologists found carefully carved stone points with fluted faces. The earliest, which may be 11,500 years old, are called Clovis points because they were first discovered near Clovis, New Mexico. Clovis points are sharp-edged, flat stones between three and nine inches long. Paleo-Indian toolmakers fluted the points, flaking off thin slivers of stone to form grooves on both sides of each point.

To make a spear, the Indians split the end of a long piece of wood and slipped the point into it. The flutes helped hold the point in place. Strong cords were used to tie the point to the shaft. This type of spear

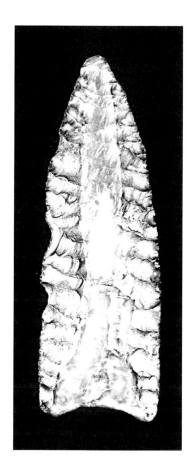

Clovis points, such as this one found in Nebraska, were fluted so that the groove on each side of the point would help hold it in the split end of a spear shaft.

was the deadliest weapon of its age. Hunters either stabbed their prey repeatedly or threw their spears from a distance, using wooden or bone spear-throwers to increase the speed and killing force of the spears.

Most of these ancient spearheads were made of a stone called chert. But sometimes Paleo-Indians made points from beautiful stones like jasper, chalcedony, and transparent rock crystal, which were more difficult to carve than chert. These points have been found hundreds of miles from the sources of their stones, leading archaeologists to conclude that Paleo-Indians traded the points or gave them as gifts.

Different types of archaeological sites show other details of Paleo-Indian life. A hilltop site containing only hunting tools might have been a hunting camp from which men could look out over water holes or animal trails. Small sites with only food-preparation tools were probably places where teams of women collected and prepared wild plants for food. Large sites with many hearths and a variety of tools might have been favorite campsites that were used frequently over a number of years.

From the debris left at these sites, archaeologists estimate that each band had between 15 and 50 members. These groups

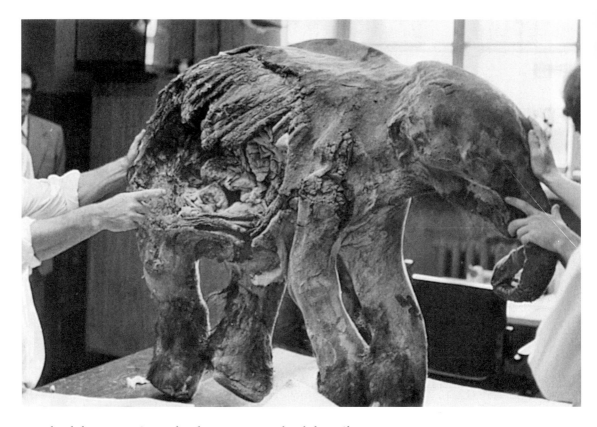

probably consisted of an extended family or a few related families. It is likely that they became friends with other groups so that they could arrange marriages for their young people and share food during hard times. Bands may also have joined forces to form hunting parties to attack whole herds of animals. Working in large groups, hunters caused herds to stampede off a cliff or into a closed canyon where the animals could be killed more easily.

Unfortunately, many aspects of the Paleo-

Paleo-Indians survived the Ice Age by hunting large animals such as the wooly mammoth. This baby mammoth, which lived 10,000 years ago, was found frozen during an excavation in Siberia.

Indians' way of life can not be understood from the clues they left behind. Because they were always on the move, they accumulated few objects. Little trace is left of their homes. Most likely, they camped out under animal skins spread over branches or large bones. Paleo-Indians also lived in rock shelters, where rock overhangs protected them from bad weather. Since almost no artwork or burial remains have been unearthed, little can be learned about their religious beliefs.

Although many questions about the early Native Americans remain unanswered, archaeologists have been able to trace their paths as they spread across North and South America. As groups moved into different environments, such as deserts, prairies, and forests, they began to develop the many distinct cultures that Europeans encountered when they reached the Americas. ▲

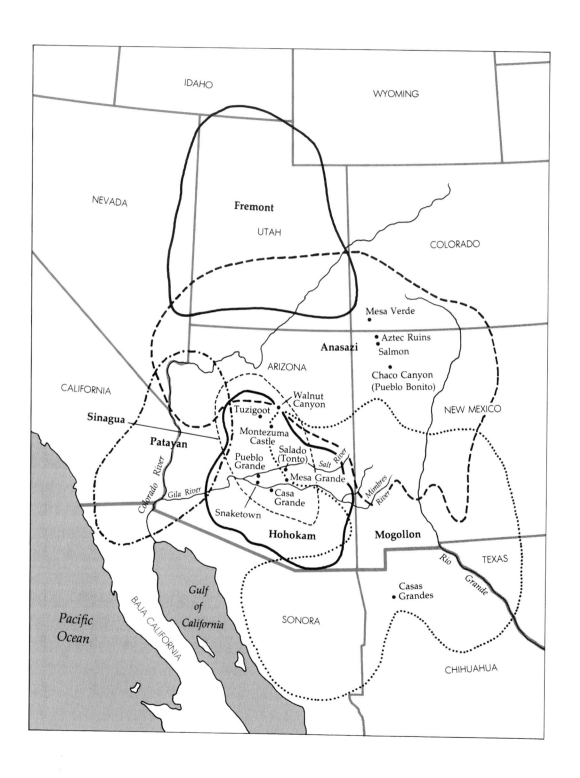

As prehistoric peoples spread across North America, they developed many different cultures to adapt to their varied environments. This map shows the major cultural areas of the early Native Americans.

CHAPTER 3

Adapting to New Environments

The end of the Ice Age changed North America in ways that brought the Paleo-Indian lifestyle to a halt. Cold-loving mammoths—the main targets of Paleo-Indian spears—disappeared even more completely than the glaciers. By 7000 B.C. they were extinct, victims of both environmental change and overeager hunters.

More than 30 types of mammals died out during the thousands of years of global warming that ended the Ice Age. Many

27

were large species—a few weighed in at four or five tons. Scientists do not know why so many animals did not survive, but the changing climate probably played a major role in their extinction.

Without these large mammals to hunt, people began pursuing smaller game, such as rabbits and birds, and catching fish. They gathered seeds from wild plants and ground off the tough husks with stones. A new hunting and foraging tradition, which archaeologists call Archaic, replaced Paleo-Indian big game hunting. The Archaic tradition lasted from around 8000 B.C. to 1000 B.C.

Warmer weather transformed the North American landscape. Across vast stretches of the east, melting glaciers left behind clay, sand, and gravel that slowly turned to soil. Trees and other plants took root. Spruce, pine, and fir trees spread throughout the cold northern and mountainous areas; maple and beech trees flourished in the moderate climate of the northeast; while oak, chestnut, and tulip trees took over the warmer south.

Pollen grains trapped in bogs many thousands of years ago reveal that *forestation* was a long, gradual process. Throughout the eastern United States and into Canada, from the Mississippi River to the Atlantic Ocean, open grasslands gave way to forests. Archaeologists call this region the Eastern Woodlands.

The woodlands attracted a richer variety of plants and animals than had the earlier grasslands. Archaic Indians here found that they no longer had to pursue herds of wild animals over a wide range. In the lush forest they could hunt deer; gather nuts, berries, and roots; and fish in streams and lakes, all within a small territory.

Hunter-gatherers of the Eastern Woodlands learned to take advantage of the fact that certain plants and animals flourished in the same areas year after year. The Indians could schedule their travels accordingly, returning to the best sources of food for each season. A band might catch fish in a favorite stream every spring, gather fruit in a certain meadow every summer, and hunt deer in a particular woods every fall. Since the forests provided a more abundant and varied diet than had earlier environments, bands grew larger and more self-sufficient. Long-distance contacts with other bands, which was common during Paleo-Indian times, became unnecessary.

The Eastern Woodlands embraced many environments, and each group of Indians adapted to its particular surroundings. In oak forests, Indians learned how to process acorns to make a nutritious flour. Along rivers, Indians devised nets and weirs (fences built in streams) to catch fish. In the lake-dotted northern woods, Indians used birch bark to build canoes that were light enough to carry between bodies of water. By the end of the Archaic period, each region had its own distinctive tools and way of life. And as the people of each region coined new words and phrases, new languages were born. The many languages spoken in the Eastern Woodlands when the Europeans arrived probably got their start during the Archaic period.

The Archaic Indians began to develop ways to increase the amount of fruits and vegetables that grew in their territory. For example, they discovered that plants produced more food when they were harvested regularly. The Indians also burned off unwanted plants to clear land for useful ones like sunflowers and squash. By 2500 B.C. some Archaic Indians were planting seeds and cuttings to raise some of their food. However, they did not yet settle down in permanent villages to farm.

The late Archaic Indians of the Eastern Woodlands were so successful at foraging

People who lived in the Great Lakes area engraved this shell gorget about 3,000 years ago. Gorgets were ornaments that were worn on a band around the neck. The animal on this gorget might be a bear cub.

and gardening that they had surplus food to store for less plentiful times. They developed pottery to provide containers for the ample provisions. Food storage brought an important social change. Local bands joined forces to preserve and store their extra food, forming tribes to protect their supplies from other groups.

When the Indians lived in small bands, everyone could share in decision making. But as groups grew larger—to 500 or more members—leaders were needed. For even larger groups to function as a whole, power had to be distributed among leaders of different ranks. By the end of the Archaic period, Indians in the Eastern Woodlands were living as members of tribes with formal leaders.

Farther west, an entirely different environment developed in the region between the Rocky Mountains and the mountain chain formed by the Sierra Nevada and the Cascade ranges. The tall peaks to the east and west cut off this area from moist winds blowing off the Pacific Ocean and the Gulf of Mexico, so little rain fell. Warmer weather melted the ice sheets, but the lakes and marshlands that were left by the retreating glaciers grew more and more salty as the

The desert climate preserves objects that would have decayed long ago in wetter regions. This basket full of corn kernels was discovered at Pueblo Bonito, New Mexico, in 1895.

water evaporated into the hot air. Many dried up completely, creating an area known as the Desert West.

As in the Eastern Woodlands, during the Archaic period Indians in the Desert West turned to hunting smaller game and depending more on plants for food. But the region became so dry that only small bands of hunter-gatherers eked out an existence there. Migrating between stream- or lakeside camps and mountain slopes, they lived on fish and waterbirds, small mammals, piñon nuts, rushes and grasses, and cactus fruits.

In the Great Basin—the driest part of the Desert West—archaeologists have found caves where Indians camped and stored tools and food. The dry climate has preserved their inventive gear. They wove baskets (possibly the first in the world), carved wooden bowls, and knotted rushes into sandals. Evidence of their largely vegetarian diet includes sickles for cutting plants, stones for grinding seeds into flour, and digging sticks for harvesting roots. They still hunted with stone-tipped spears, but they also made nets and traps for birds, rodents, and fish.

In 1924, an archaeologist made an amazing discovery in a cave in northwestern

Nevada—a 2,000-year-old basket filled with duck decoys. Hunters made the decoys by forming reeds into the shape of a duck, then painting them and covering them with duck feathers to make them look like living birds. These decoys floated on lakes and lured ducks to a spot where they could be caught by hunters who were hiding nearby.

The American landscape changed least in the Great Plains. Here, Indians continued to follow herds of large grazing animals over open grasslands. Now they aimed at bison instead of mammoths, but their tool kits and lifestyles remained much the same.

At the peak of the warming, however, during a long dry period some 7,000 years ago, the Great Plains dried up. The drought lasted about 2,500 years. Larger bison died off for lack of grass, and the smaller, modern species evolved.

Little remains of the hardy folk who weathered the dry spell. Using sticks that were hardened by fire, they tapped water under dry lake beds by digging wells, some as deep as 10 feet. They moved frequently between well sites up to 100 miles apart. Finding water became more vital than hunting bison. Until the drought ended around 2500 B.C. and the herds of smaller bison increased, the Plains Indians' principal rations were cactus fruits, wild grasses, lizards, snakes, and the occasional pronghorn antelope.

For most of North America, the Archaic period was a time of increasing diversity. Indians separated into groups that developed independently of each other. Although still nomadic, they traveled over smaller areas, occasionally trading with their neighbors, but rarely over long distances. Each group devised the equipment necessary to take advantage of the resources of its environment. Gradually, Native Americans were becoming many different peoples, all closely tied to their natural surroundings ▲

The Anasazi people of the Southwest lived in apartment complexes called pueblos. The ruins pictured here are in Mesa Verde National Park in Colorado.

CHAPTER 4

Foraging and Farming in the West

By the time Europeans arrived in North America, most of the Indians they encountered were farmers. But along the West Coast, many peoples still foraged, fished, and hunted. They lived on wild foods not because they were more primitive than their neighbors to the east but because the land and the ocean were so bountiful that farming was not necessary. These peoples did not have to search far or migrate each season to find what they needed. Instead they settled into communities and simply gathered food practically from their doorsteps.

Early peoples who reached the Pacific Coast north of Mexico found a climate that ranged from hot and dry in the south to cool and wet in the north. Tall mountain ranges—the Sierra Nevada and the Cascade Mountains—separated this coastal strip from the Desert West. Between the mountains and the sea lay highlands, valleys, and a lower mountain range along the coast. Many different regions existed side by side, including thick redwood forests, open oak parklands, and deserts.

Bands of hunters and foragers came to California from every overland direction over a long period of time. Like other Indians during the Archaic period, each group adapted to its particular environment. These Indians grew so adept at exploiting the resources of their surroundings that they had surpluses which they could trade. By A.D. 500, about 500 small tribes inhabited California, all specializing in different products. People made fishing nets, sealskins, beads, baskets, tools, or canoes, each group working with the resources at hand and trading with other groups.

The California Indians' trading network was so complex that it needed money to work smoothly. Indians living on the Channel Islands off the coast of southern

California made the money from a certain type of seashell. They chipped the shells into disks, fired them in hot coals, pierced them with a stone awl, and strung them into strands long enough to wrap once around a person's hand. With this shell currency, Indians bought goods from other places.

North of California, the land along the Pacific coast was less diverse but richer. The range of mountains along the coast trapped the moist air coming off the northern Pacific Ocean, creating a cool rain forest. This area, known as the Northwest Coast, stretches from northern California,

This cedarwood bowl was made in the 19th century by the Kwakiutl people of the Northwest Coast. Items such as this were often given away at ceremonies called potlatches.

across Oregon, Washington, and British Columbia, Canada, to southern Alaska.

The Paleo-Indians who settled along the Northwest Coast discovered a land of plenty. Rivers teemed with salmon and other migrating fish. The woods abounded in moose, deer, and bear. Sheep and goats clambered over the rocky mountainsides, and seals, whales, and shellfish filled the ocean.

Giant cedar trees provided wood for houses, canoes, storage boxes, totem poles, and ceremonial masks. The strong fibers of cedar bark were woven into blankets, mats, and baskets. Mountain sheep supplied wool for clothing and horns that were carved to make spoons and bowls. The Indians fashioned fishing nets from seaweed and hammered copper nuggets into jewelry.

Surrounded by natural riches and having no need to trade for goods from other areas, the Indians of the Northwest settled down to enjoy their wealth. Food was easy to come by. Two weeks of hard work catching and preserving salmon could feed a large village for several months. More salmon would be leaping upstream long before the supply ran out.

continued on page 49

BURIED TREASURES

Archaeologists have learned much about the lives of early Native Americans by examining the objects, called artifacts, that they left behind. Many of the items uncovered from the earth, such as pottery, tools, and jewelry, are made of clay, stone, and metal. People living in North America used these materials to make objects for cooking, clothing, and shelter. Often, they took such care in decorating practical objects that today, hundreds of years later, we still appreciate their beauty.

Archaeologists are not always certain about how each piece was used or what it meant to the people who made it. But by studying the materials and techniques they used, we can learn much about a way of life that developed in North America over thousands of years.

Mogollon tradition bowl and jar, black and white paint on red clay. Women were traditionally the potters among the American Indians.

Mimbres bowl with parrot design from Hawikuh, whose people may have been ancestors of the Zuni Pueblo people. Hawikuh is in New Mexico, a few miles from Zuni, near the Arizona border.

Mimbres bowls. The Mogollon people living in the Mimbres valley of New Mexico were superb potters.

A classic black-on-white Mimbres bowl. Bats often appear on Mimbres pottery.

A Mogollon jar. Indian women did not have pottery wheels and shaped their pots by hand.

Hohokam jars, in the style archaeologists call Sacaton red-on-
buff. The Hohokam people cremated their dead and interred
the ashes in pottery jars with in-
verted bowls for covers.

Anasazi bowl. Several Anasazi
pueblos, some containing
hundreds of rooms, fill Chaco
Canyon in northern New
Mexico.

Hohokam pottery in a variety of shapes. Pottery of this tradition is
characterized by strong patterns and dramatic forms. The pottery
forms often present broad surfaces for decoration, usually geometric.

Embossed copper portrait with such typical Southern Cult features as an ear spool and forked eye design.

Figures of a kneeling woman and man, about two feet tall, carved from solid blocks of marble. They were found with the remains of four burials in a mound in Etowah, Georgia, a large community that is one of the best-known sites of the late Mississippian Southern Cult tradition.

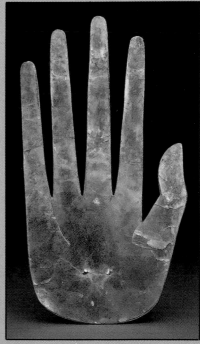

Hand, cut from mica, 28 centimeters (10 inches) long, from a Hopewell site in Ohio.

This stone beaver is a Hopewell platform pipe bowl; there is a hole in his back for tobacco.

This wooden figure from Key Marco off the Florida coast may represent a cougar deity or a human wearing a cat disguise.

continued from page 40

The ease of food gathering left time for the development of a complex society with elaborate arts, crafts, rituals, and ceremonies. Different groups, led by chiefs, competed to see who could accumulate the most goods. Occasionally war broke out, usually over territory such as a good fishing site.

Members of each group were ranked according to their kinship to the chief. Much of the artwork of the Northwest Coast displays symbols of social rank, such as family crests and titles. Ceremonies often featured masked dancers performing a legend about a family's origins. Some of these masks were so elaborate that they contained a second face inside the first. By pulling hidden strings, the wearer could be transformed into a different character.

The importance of wealth as a status symbol led to the development of a gift-giving ceremony called a potlatch. A wealthy man would host a potlatch, during which feasting, religious ceremonies, and dance performances filled several days. The host gave away finely woven blankets, fur robes, shell necklaces, wooden armor, and ornately carved bowls to his guests. With this lavish display of wealth, the host increased his prestige in the community and proved himself worthy of his status.

Far to the south, very different types of communities flourished. Unlike the California and Northwest Coast Indians, the Indians of the Southwest lived in a dry environment with few food resources. Only by growing much of their food could people here settle down to live in one place. Three major cultural traditions developed in the Southwest. They are known as Hohokam, Mogollon (MO-go-yon), and Anasazi (an-ah-ZAH-zee).

Archaeologists believe that corn, squash, and beans first arrived in the Southwest from Mexico about 2,000 to 4,000 years ago. These three crops became the basis of all North American Indian agriculture. Often called the "three sisters," corn, squash, and beans made a nutritionally complete diet. By growing these foods, the Indian population became less dependent on hunting and foraging. As in the Eastern Woodlands, plant cultivation in the Southwest began gradually, with wild resources such as piñon nuts and game supplementing the diet.

When the southwestern climate turned drier about 2,000 years ago, farmers had to find ways to bring water to their crops. In the Sonoran Desert of southern Arizona, the Hohokam tapped the Salt and Gila rivers to *irrigate* their fields. At first the fields were close to the riverbank, and water was diverted from the river through small ditches. By A.D. 700, the Hohokam were digging canals six or seven feet deep and lining them with clay to keep the water from seeping into the ground. Water traveled through a network of ditches to fields up to 30 miles away. In the area of Phoenix, Arizona, archaeologists have uncovered at least 360 miles of irrigation canals.

Hohokam farmers grew two crops a year. They timed their planting to take advantage of spring and summer rains in the mountains of eastern Arizona, which raised water levels in the rivers. Despite this complex irrigation system, however, the desert environment was too uncertain for the Hohokam to rely completely on farming. In years of low rainfall, little water reached the canals. So the Hohokam continued to gather mesquite pods and cactus fruits and to hunt rabbit and deer.

The Hohokam settled into communities near their irrigated fields. They lived in pit houses, which were built in dug-out depressions in the ground so that part of the structure was below the surface. Walls and roofs were constructed of wooden poles with clay filling the chinks. Influenced by their

contacts with the Indians of Mexico, the Hohokam built large oval ball courts and low earthen platforms—possibly for temples—in their larger settlements. Each large town probably controlled the smaller villages around it, forming a governing structure known as a chiefdom. The remains of some of these towns, such as Mesa Grande, Pueblo Grande, and Snaketown, can still be seen in Arizona.

Archaeologists have found much evidence of Mexico's influence on Hohokam

This Hohokam ball court discovered in Snaketown, Arizona, was made more than a thousand years ago.

culture. Mexican traders brought small cop-per bells and rubber balls to Hohokam vil-lages.   Hohokam potters used Mexican designs on some of their buff-colored pots, which they decorated with a darker red-orange clay.   Hohokam artists made elaborate ornaments out of seashells from the Gulf of California. They cut them into beads, pendants, or bracelets, or they etched designs on them, using the juice of the saguaro fruit.

The Hohokam chiefdoms collapsed by the middle of the 15th century, defeated by either crop failures or Apache raids from the north. Survivors retreated to small, scatter-ed villages. The Pima Alto and Papago Indi-ans, who live in Arizona today, are probably their descendants. In the Pima language, Hohokam means "those who have gone."

To the east of the Hohokam, in the moun-tains near the border of Arizona and New Mexico, the Mogollon tradition began around A.D. 250. Like the Hohokam, the Mogollon built pit houses, digging down into the ground for insulation against the hot days and cold nights of the desert. Early Mogollon villages sat atop mesas (flat-topped hills), perhaps for protection from attack. Crops were grown in the river valleys below.

The Mogollon made distinctive pottery with geometric, human, and animal designs. The best-known Mogollon pottery is found along the Mimbres River in New Mexico, where potters painted black designs on white pots. The Mogollon often placed pottery in graves, "killing" the pots and bowls by breaking or piercing them before burying them with the dead.

Mogollon culture expanded over a wide area during the 9th to the 11th centuries, spreading southward into the Mexican states of Chihuahua and Sonora. At Casas Grandes, in Chihuahua, and at other sites built after A.D. 1000, the Mogollon built above-ground houses that were clustered together into apartment complexes.

In these complexes, extended families lived together in groups of apartments. The Mogollon traced their family relations through women, so an extended family would include a group of related women and their husbands and children. Underground chambers called kivas provided space for related men to meet together. Each village also contained one larger kiva, called a great kiva, that served as a ceremonial center for the whole community.

Mogollon culture, like the Hohokam, declined before the arrival of the Spanish.

Archaeologists speculate that this was caused either by warfare or by a severe famine. Those Mogollon who survived may have joined the Hohokam or the Anasazi. Some modern-day Zuni Indians are descendants of the Mogollon.

The third major tradition of the prehistoric Southwest, the Anasazi (which means "the ancient ones" in the Navajo language), first appeared about 2,000 years ago in the Four Corners area, where the borders of Utah, New Mexico, Arizona, and Colorado meet. Still living partly nomadic lives, the Anasazi stored their goods in caves while hunting and foraging for food. Archaeologists called the early Anasazi "Basketmakers" because many skillfully woven baskets were found among the artifacts in these caves.

By the 5th century, the Anasazi began to settle down in pit houses, some so deep as to be completely underground. After A.D. 700, they developed their own pottery, patterned after Hohokam and Mogollon styles, and started building many-storied houses above ground out of stone and adobe. These compact apartment complexes are now called pueblos (from the Spanish word for town). The most dramatic were constructed high on the sides of mesas, under large rock overhangs. One of these complexes, which is preserved in Colorado's Mesa Verde National Park, contains more than 200 rooms and 23 underground kivas.

The Anasazi expanded across New Mexico and Colorado, building many pueblos linked by an amazing network of roads 30 feet wide. Twelve impressive Anasazi towns line Chaco Canyon in New Mexico. Each town was designed in the shape of a giant D and contained several hundred rooms, arranged in tiers four stories high around a central plaza. A great kiva usually dominated the plaza, and smaller kivas were buried in front of the curved line of rooms.

The largest town in Chaco Canyon, Pueblo Bonito, had 650 to 800 rooms and covered three acres. Some 1,200 people lived there during the 12th century. Using dendrochronology to date the large wooden beams used in the roofing, archaeologists have determined that Pueblo Bonito was constructed between 919 and 1085. The Indians carried these logs to Chaco Canyon from wooded areas 47 miles away.

Around 1300, the Anasazi began to abandon many of their villages, and their population declined. Some archaeologists believe this was caused by a disastrous drought, which was recorded in tree rings for the years 1276 to 1299. Perhaps raids by nomads or internal quarrels contributed to the decline of the Anasazi culture. By the time Spanish explorers reached the area, only small communities of Anasazi remained.   They survive today as the Pueblo Indians.

The Southwest remains a rich source of information for archaeologists.   The prehistoric Indians of the area built homes that still stand, and the dry climate has preserved many artifacts. Archaeologists may some day find evidence to explain why these impressive cultures declined centuries ago. ▲

The mounds built by the Adena people still mark the landscape of the Ohio River valley. This remarkable mound in Ohio is 1,330 feet long and is shaped like a giant serpent.

CHAPTER 5

Urban Living in the East

About 3,000 years ago, at the end of the Archaic period, Indians in the Eastern Woodlands began settling in villages and forming tribes ruled by chiefs. Evidence found in the graves of these peoples indicates that they had a complex society with different social classes.

The Adena (ah-DEE-nah) people, who lived in the Ohio River valley between 700 B.C. and A.D. 400, were among the first to build tall, cone-shaped mounds to bury their dead. Inside the mounds, some of the dead were placed in log tombs or clay-lined basins. Their bodies were painted with red or black pigment and surrounded by stone pipes, engraved stone tablets, and jewelry made of copper, mica, and seashells.

But not everyone received such elaborate burials. Many of the dead were cremated and placed in simpler graves within the mound. These distinctions reflect differences in social status within the community.

The Adena built hundreds of burial mounds, most of them in the central Ohio Valley. One of the largest mounds was 240 feet in diameter and 70 feet high. To construct it, the Adena piled up 72,000 tons of earth, basketful by basketful.

The Adena also built large earthen enclosures around or near their burial mounds, perhaps to set them apart as sacred ground. The Adena probably gathered at these sites for religious ceremonies. Some of the earthworks were shaped like animals. Serpent Mound in Ohio is a 1,200-foot-long snake that rises four to five feet above the ground.

The pipes found in Adena burial mounds reveal that tobacco-smoking rituals were already part of North American Indian life and that Adena Indians practiced shamanism. Shamans were people, usually men, who were believed to have supernatural powers. The Adena believed that shamans could leave their bodies and become animals when under the influence of tobacco or some other drug. Often shamans were healers and spiritual leaders of their community.

Items found in graves also show that the Adena engaged in long-distance trade. Copper came from northern Michigan, mica from the Appalachian Mountains, and shells from the Atlantic seaboard. But this trade differed from the trading of Paleo-Indian times. Paleo-Indians exchanged practical items that were already formed, such as spear tips. The Adena instead acquired raw materials and used them to produce luxury goods such as bracelets, beads, rings, and neck ornaments called gorgets.

Another culture that flourished in Ohio built even larger earthworks and had more elaborate burials than the Adena. The Hopewell surrounded their burial mounds with earthen ridges, some more than 1,600 feet in diameter. The dead were buried with valuable objects such as copper tools and ornaments, bone and antler carvings coated with thin layers of gold or silver foil, crystal charms, mica cutouts, and animal teeth. The Hopewell also made fine pottery and clay figurines that show how people dressed and wore their hair. Stone carvers created beautiful objects, including pipes with bowls shaped like animals.

The Hopewell created a vast trade network that covered much of the present-day United States and Canada. From the many tribes in this network the Hopewell received the materials they needed to create their luxury items. For example, obsidian (volcanic glass) and grizzly bear teeth came from the Rocky Mountains, and shark and alligator jaws came from the Gulf Coast. In exchange for the items they traded to the Hopewell, these tribes received Hopewell artworks.

The Hopewell influenced the communities with whom they traded, and mound-building spread throughout most of the Eastern Woodlands. The Effigy Mound culture in present-day Wisconsin, Minnesota, and Iowa built earthen mounds in the shapes of panthers, bears, birds, and humans. One bird-shaped mound near Madison, Wisconsin, has a wingspan of 625 feet.

By A.D. 800, the Hopewell communities had declined and a new tradition, called Mississippian, was spreading through the Eastern Woodlands. Two plant foods introduced from Mexico aided its rise. One was a variety of corn that could grow during the short northeastern growing season; the

This 11-inch-long piece of mica cut in the shape of a bird claw is one of several artworks found in Hopewell graves.

other was protein-rich Mexican beans. Now the eastern tribes could cultivate the nutritionally balanced "three sisters"—corn, squash, and beans. The Mississippian people still relied on hunting, fishing, and gathering, but farming made it possible to establish towns and cities.

Mississippian culture flourished on the *floodplains* of the Mississippi, Arkansas, Tennessee, Ohio, and Red rivers. The soil in this area was extremely *fertile* because each spring, just before planting season, the rivers flooded, carrying water and nutrients to the fields.

New tools helped increase food production. By attaching chert slabs to wooden shafts, Mississippians created hoes to clear weeds and break up the soil. The only other tool needed in the easily worked river lands was a digging stick to prepare the soil and plant seeds.

To collect and redistribute the crops, rulers built *urban* centers. The sites of Mississippian towns and cities are marked by mounds. Some were burial mounds, but others formed platforms on which the Indians built temples and other public buildings. These platform mounds were possibly inspired by the pyramids of Mexican civilizations.

An Adena burial mound in Miamisburg, Ohio.

A typical Mississippian town had between 1 and 20 mounds. None of the buildings that once stood atop these mounds survives today. However, a member of Hernando de Soto's expedition to North America in 1539 to 1541 described one of the temples:

> Now this temple was large, being more than a hundred feet in length and forty in width. Its walls were high . . . and its roof also was very lofty and drafty. . . . Over the roof of the temple many large and small shells of different marine animals had been arranged. . . . These shells had been placed with the inside out so as to show their greatest luster, and they included many conch shells of strange mag-

nificence.   Between them . . . were large strands (of pearls). . . . The temple was covered on the outside with all these things, and they made a splendid sight in the brilliance of the sun.

Mississippian mounds were arranged around open squares where people gathered for political and religious ceremonies. Chiefs and other important people lived in the urban centers, which were sometimes surrounded by a palisade (a tall protective fence made of logs).   Farmers and other workers lived in smaller villages nearby.

The largest prehistoric city north of Mexico was built by the Mississippians at Cahokia, Illinois.   Founded around the year 600, Cahokia grew and prospered, reaching

Mississippians built temples atop flat-topped mounds. Temples were made of wooden poles covered with mats of grass, and some were surrounded by posts on which were carved the faces of gods. A stairway made of logs led up to the temple.

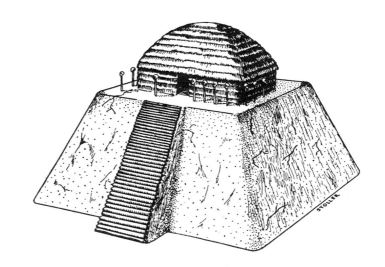

its peak around 1200.   More than 100 mounds of different sizes and shapes remain at Cahokia today. The largest, called Monks Mound, covers some 16 acres (the equivalent of 30 football fields) and is 100 feet tall (as high as a 10-story building). A temple once stood atop the mound. Archaeologists disagree about the number of people who lived in and around Cahokia at its peak. The population may have been anywhere between 10,000 and 75,000.

This Mississippian shell carving was discovered in a burial mound near Spiro, Oklahoma.

Other major Mississippian cities flourished in present-day Moundville, Alabama; Spiro, Oklahoma; and Etowah, Georgia. People from smaller towns gathered in the cities to take part in religious ceremonies and to trade.   There was also a thriving trade between urban centers.   Both raw materials and finished goods traveled long distances along the network of rivers. Traders carried shells from the Atlantic Ocean and the Gulf of Mexico as far inland as Oklahoma.

The Mississippians created impressive works of art. Seashells were carved with elaborate designs, such as an eye in the palm of an open hand, a weeping eye, intricate crosses, and sunbursts. Some of these designs were also carved in wood and stone, painted on cloth, and embossed on sheets of copper. Mississippian potters were influenced by Mexican pottery, producing long-necked water jars and pots shaped like human heads.

By the time Europeans arrived in North America, most Mississippian centers had declined. For unknown reasons, city life had become undesirable, and people had settled in smaller villages. Some archaeologists think that food shortages were the cause. Others believe that diseases spread rapidly in the heavily populated towns, causing many people to move away.

Several Mississippian centers prospered well into the 16th and 17th centuries. However, European explorers brought new diseases that killed much of the population. By the late 18th and early 19th centuries, when American settlers began moving into the former territory of the Adena, Hopewell, and Mississippian people, the only visible evidence of these impressive civilizations was the mounds. Not until the 20th century were archaeologists able to piece together the history and the way of life of the people who had built them. ▲

The Inuits mastered the
harsh weather conditions
of the Arctic. In the center
is a shaman, a person
who communicates with
the spirit world.

CHAPTER 6

Conquering the Arctic

The last Native Americans to arrive in North America were the ancestors of the Inuit and the Aleut. (The Inuit are also called Eskimos, the name given to them by the Abnaki Indians of northern Canada. The name Eskimo comes from the Abnaki word meaning "eaters of raw meat." The name Inuit means "the people" in the Inuit language.)

The physical characteristics and languages of the Inuit and Aleut show that they are more closely related to the people of northeast Asia than are other Native Americans. This indicates that they migrated from Asia long after the

Paleo-Indians. They probably reached Alaska around 4,000 years ago.

No one knows exactly how these Arctic hunters came to North America. Perhaps they walked across the pack ice that sometimes bridges the 56-mile-wide Bering Strait. Or they might have journeyed across the strait in boats made of animal skins. However they traveled, these bold immigrants were not intimidated by what one writer has called "one of the most unpromising and demanding environments ever inhabited by man."

Much of the American Arctic lies north of the Arctic Circle, where there are winter days when the sun never rises and summer nights when the sun does not set. But the American Arctic also includes the tundra that stretches across western and northern Alaska, northern Canada, and Greenland. Tundra is treeless land that is frozen for most of the year. During the short Arctic summers, the surface of the tundra thaws and some small plants are able to grow, but there is a permanently frozen layer beneath the surface.

Winters in the American Arctic are eight to nine months long, with temperatures that can reach -80 degrees Fahrenheit. In the summer, temperatures average only 50

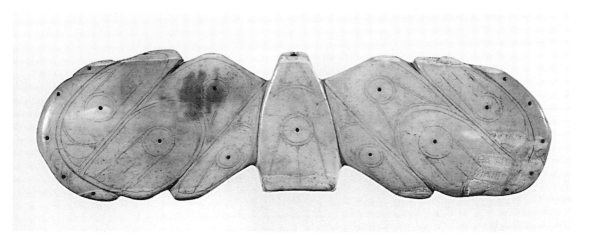

This bird-shaped piece of walrus ivory was found on St. Lawrence Island in Alaska. Archaeologists believe that prehistoric hunters might have attached it to the shaft of a harpoon.

degrees Fahrenheit. Large herds of caribou and musk oxen as well as countless tiny voles and lemmings graze on low grasses, mosses, and dwarf willows. The many small rodents provide food for foxes, wolves, and weasels. Bays and inlets on the edges of the tundra create thousands of miles of coastline inhabited by sea mammals such as walruses and seals. The northern seas attract many varieties of whales, and the rivers and lakes support fish and ducks.

Around 2000 B.C. the newcomers settled along the Alaskan coast and the Aleutian Islands, hunting seals and caribou and catching salmon. At first they depended on nearby forests for firewood and for timber to build homes. But as these people spread eastward, they developed the tools they needed to harvest the resources of the Arctic Ocean and to survive the bitter winters.

Dogs were domesticated for use as hunting aids, and perhaps for food. Stone lamps that burned whale or seal oil replaced wood fires. By 1500 B.C. the bow and arrow had been added to the growing arsenal of hunting tools. Arctic excavations have also turned up specialized harpoons and hooks for various animals and fish, spear-throwers custom-made for individual hunters, bow drills, snow shovels, knives, and whetstones for sharpening tools.

The early Arctic dwellers invented specialized gear to cope with their snowy environment. Ice creepers were carved from bone and ivory and attached to boot soles to enable people to walk in slippery conditions. Whalebones became runners for sleds. Ivory knives were used to cut blocks of snow, from which igloos were built to provide housing during winter hunts. To protect their eyes from snow blindness, hunters made snow goggles by carving eye slits in a piece of ivory and spreading soot over it to absorb light.

Among the most essential equipment was warm clothing. With bone needles and sinew thread, the northern peoples sewed skins into outfits to protect their bodies from the brutal cold. Many layers of clothing provided insulation and warmth. First came underwear made from duck skins, with the feathers still in place; then pants and parka made of caribou hide with the fur turned in. The top layer was a second looser suit of caribou hide with the fur turned out. Boots lined with moss were also worn in two layers. Waterproof clothing was made from seal or walrus intestine. When ocean hunting in small skin-covered canoes called kayaks, men kept themselves dry by fastening their outer layer of clothing to the kayak's cover, forming a watertight seal.

The most successful of the Arctic peoples, the Thule (THYOO-lee) culture, began to move eastward from Alaska about A.D. 1000. The Thule are the ancestors of the Inuit, who still live throughout the American Arctic. The Thule were the first Arctic people to train dogs to pull sleds. This innovation made it easier for them to move around carrying heavy loads, especially during winter hunting.

Around A.D. 1000, the climate of the Arctic grew milder, allowing the Thule to advance into territory that had previously been forbidding. Within a few centuries Thule culture had spread across the American Arctic, from Alaska to Greenland.

*Towana Spivey (left),
an archaeologist who
is a Native American,
supervises an excavation
at Fort Towson,
Oklahoma.*

The warming trend that led the Thule east brought other settlers to North America. Voyaging westward from Norway and Iceland, Viking explorers discovered Greenland and Newfoundland and founded colonies. Archaeological sites reveal that Vikings and Eskimos made contact in Greenland. Norse armor, woolen cloth, and iron tools have turned up in Thule houses.

When colder winters resumed in the 13th century, the Norse left Greenland and went home. However, later Europeans who reached America were more successful. As the Spanish, English, and French invaded the North American continent, the prehistory of North America came to an end.

The historical period begins with the encounter between Native American and

European cultures. Early trading brought horses, iron tools, and firearms to the Indians and tobacco, corn, and furs to the Europeans. But Europeans also brought many new diseases. Because the Indians had never been exposed to these diseases, their bodies were not able to resist them. Smallpox, measles, and the bubonic plague spread quickly through Indian villages and towns, in some places wiping out as much as 90 percent of the population.

The large number of Indian lives lost to disease made it easier for settlers from Europe to gain a foothold in America and impose their culture on it. As one archaeologist notes, "Were it not for the diseases of the 16th and 17th centuries, people in North America might today be speaking Mohawk, Ojibwa, and Nahuatl and living their lives according to Native American rather than European customs."

Today archaeologists, some themselves descended from prehistoric American Indians, continue to dig for evidence to fill in the picture of North American prehistory. Each year brings exciting new discoveries that expand our knowledge of the diverse prehistoric peoples who once lived in North America. ▲

GLOSSARY

archaeologist   a person who pieces together the history and way of life of ancient peoples by studying the objects they created, such as tools, artwork, and buildings

culture   the customary practices and beliefs of a group of people

excavation   the uncovering of ancient artifacts through careful, orderly digging

fertile   able to support abundant plant life

floodplain   level land that is often flooded by a nearby river

forestation   the slow, gradual creation of forests

geology   a science that deals with the history of the earth as recorded in rocks

glaciers   huge masses of ice that build up in cold regions and on mountaintops

hunter-gatherers   people who live by hunting animals and gathering wild plants; this way of life was common before the development of farming

irrigate   to bring water to fields through ditches, pipes, or other man-made structures

magnetic field   The area affected by the pull of a magnet; the center of the earth creates a magnetic field that extends thousands of miles into space.

nomads   people who have no permanent home and are continually moving to find sources of food

sinew   tough fibers that attach muscle to bone; Native Americans used animal sinew as thread for sewing

urban   characteristic of city life

CHRONOLOGY

1.7 million–10,000 years ago	Pleistocene Epoch, or Ice Age
25,000–14,000 years ago	Low sea levels expose Beringia, the land bridge that connected Asia and America; the ancestors of the Native Americans cross Beringia to reach Alaska
11,500–10,000 years ago	Paleo-Indian hunting bands spread across the Americas
10,000–3,000 years ago	Large Ice Age mammals die out; Archaic Indians begin hunting smaller game and gathering wild plants, developing different cultures to adapt to varied environments
4,000 years ago	The ancestors of the Inuits and Aleuts reach Alaska
2,700–1,200 years ago	Adena and Hopewell cultures thrive in the Eastern Woodlands, building burial mounds and developing long-distance trade networks
2,000–500 years ago	Hohokam, Mogollon, and Anasazi peoples farm the Southwest
1,200 years ago	Indians in the East acquire fast-ripening corn, which allows them to farm and to settle down in villages
1,200–400 years ago	Mississippian people build cities along eastern rivers and construct temple mounds
1,000 years ago	Thule Eskimos spread across the American Arctic
500 years ago	European explorers reach North America, bringing the prehistoric period to an end

INDEX

ABOUT THE AUTHOR

DIANA CHILDRESS was born in Texas and grew up in Mexico. She now lives in New York City with her husband and two daughters. As a freelance writer she has published many articles on history in magazines for young people. She has also written on historical topics for social studies textbooks.

PICTURE CREDITS

COLOR PHOTO SECTION